WITHDRAWN

GETTING A JOB IN
HAIR CARE
AND MAKEUP

BRIDGET HEOS

ROSEN
PUBLISHING®

NEW YORK

Published in 2014 by The Rosen Publishing Group, Inc.
29 East 21st Street, New York, NY 10010

Library of Congress Cataloging-in-Publication Data

Heos, Bridget.
Getting a job in hair care and makeup/by Bridget Heos.—1st ed.—
New York: Rosen, © 2014
p. cm.—(Job basics: getting the job you need)
Includes bibliographical references and index.
ISBN 978-1-4488-9611-0
1. Hairdressing—Vocational guidance—Juvenile literature. 2. Barbering—
Vocational guidance—Juvenile literature. 3. Beauty operators—
Juvenile literature. 4. Barbers—Juvenile literature. I. Title.
TT958.H46 2014
646.724 H41

Manufactured in the United States of America

CPSIA Compliance Information: Batch #S13YA: For further information, contact Rosen Publishing, New York, New York, at
1-800-237-9932.

CONTENTS

INTRODUCTION

Laurie Ramirez couldn't believe she finally had a job in makeup. She had been practicing since she was a little girl, when she would tape pictures of models to her mirror and copy their makeup to a T. Now it was her first day at an Estée Lauder makeup counter. She was setting out her products when a woman approached the counter wanting a makeover. Laurie could tell what colors would look best on her. She knew how to make her eyes "pop." Still, she was nervous. In high school, Laurie had given makeovers to classmates, especially those who needed a pick-me-up. But now it was her job. Did she have what it took to be a professional makeup artist? She performed the makeover and nervously awaited the woman's response. When the customer saw herself in the mirror, she was thrilled. She bought many of the products Laurie had used.

Laurie sought additional training through her employer each month and learned as much about the products as she could. Eventually, she went to work for another brand. Then she started her own business. Laurie talked to photographers who shot photos for magazines and advertisement. She did the makeup for the models. She put these photographs in a portfolio to show potential clients. She also built a Web site and Facebook page to show her work. She was referred to new clients by old clients for being talented and professional and a fast worker. Sometimes she worked directly for a client. Other

Makeup artists often get their start at department store counters. They give customers makeovers and sell brand-name products. Customers seek makeup-artists for on-stage or on-air performances, for special events, or for a pick-me up.

times, she worked for another makeup artist who needed extra help. Soon, Laurie was also doing makeup for television commercials, music videos, fashion shows, and NFL cheerleaders. On weekends, she did makeup for wedding parties.

She still taped professional photos to the mirror and practiced the makeup. Now, the photos were of models with special effects makeup. Laurie wanted to be able to say yes if clients asked for dramatic or scary makeup. She also thought it was fun to learn new things in her field. She even spent her free time giving her daughter and her friends makeovers.

Laurie learned makeup artistry by practicing at home. Then, she researched available jobs, applied, and attended interviews. Once she landed a job, she worked hard and never stopped learning. When the time was right, she took her career to the next level by starting her own business. These steps may sound overwhelming right now, but by acquiring some basic social and professional skills and following the tips outlined here, you, too, will soon be reporting for work at your dream job, whether that's hair styling, makeup artistry, or a related field.

Surveying the Field

Many men and women have their hair cut, styled, and colored professionally so there are many jobs available in this field. Starting out, you may be an apprentice or assistant, or a stylist at a salon that hires employees (as opposed to renting booths to stylists). Later, you may work as a senior stylist or manager at a salon, rent your own booth at a salon, or even open your own salon or barbershop. Some hair stylists also specialize in hair styling for magazines, television, movies, or live shows.

State boards of barbering and cosmetology may require apprentice hours in addition to schooling. In Hawaii, for instance, you must apprentice as a hairstylist for forty-two months and as a barber for about a year in order to earn a license. Apprentices work under an experienced hairstylist or barber. They learn the trade while getting paid a modest salary. In some ways, your job will be similar to the assistant position described below. However, you'll also get experience cutting and styling hair. If you do a good job as an apprentice, you may be offered a job at the end of your training.

As an assistant, you may work at the front desk, handle retail sales, launder the towels, tidy the booths, and prepare clients for appointments by shampooing their hair. For this reason, the job title is sometimes shampooer. You will likely have daily tasks but will also be on call for whatever the stylists need. Expect to work evenings and weekends, as these are peak times. As an employee, you'll earn a minimum hourly wage. If you work directly with clients, you'll also earn tips (about 2-8 percent of the hair appointment price for an assistant). If you are a full-time employee, you'll likely get health benefits and paid time off (about two weeks total). The salon may also offer a retirement plan.

The assistant tasks described above may not require a hair stylist license. However, many salons will prefer that you have one because they are training you to be a stylist eventually. As an assistant, you can work your way up to stylist within a few months or a few years. On the other hand, if you'd like to learn more about the field before going to school, you may consider being a receptionist at a salon. In this position, you would answer the phone, set appointments, greet customers, and handle customer payments.

There are also entry-level jobs for those who want to be

Hair stylists need a cosmetology license. They may start work as a hair stylist employed by a salon or as an assistant, or shampooer, at a salon.

a hairstylist right out of school. Many stores that sell beauty products also have a salon. Here, hair stylists often both cut and style hair and also do some retail sales work. This requires a hairstylist license. However, to only sell products, you don't need a license, just an understanding of the products and good people skills. In either position, you'll likely work retail hours, including evenings and weekends. You can work your way up to a manager.

Another typical starting position is being a stylist at a chain salon or barbershop. Here, you take several walk-in clients each day. A positive attitude, good listening skills, and the ability to offer quick, consistent haircuts are what companies seek. In this environment, you can work your way up to a manager as well. As a hair stylist in a salon, you may earn a wage only or a wage plus commission. That means you keep a percentage of the amount clients have paid for their appointments (typically 30–45 percent). As you build a clientele, you will earn more commission.

Later in your career, you may rent a booth or own a salon or barbershop. These positions require a loyal clientele: people who have come to trust your hairstyling skills and who enjoy your company.

Many barbers and hair stylists rent a booth at a barbershop or salon. They are paid directly by customers. In turn, they pay the shop owner monthly rent for the space.

You will likely have to work as many hours as you did in your first job, but you'll enjoy more freedom. On the other hand, you may choose to continue working for commission, as this offers training and leadership opportunities, the feeling of teamwork, and a consistent paycheck and benefits.

Jobs in Makeup

Makeup is different from hair care. Except for special occasions, most people don't have their makeup done professionally. That means many jobs in makeup involve either selling products or doing makeup for on-camera professionals. It also means that there are fewer jobs in makeup than in hair. It's a good idea to expand your options. An aesthetician certificate allows you to do makeup and some skin-care treatments, such as facials and microdermabrasion. You can work in either a salon or a doctor's office. A certificate in a related category, such as nail technology or cosmetology (hair

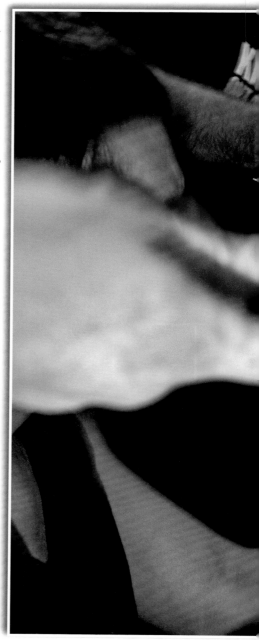

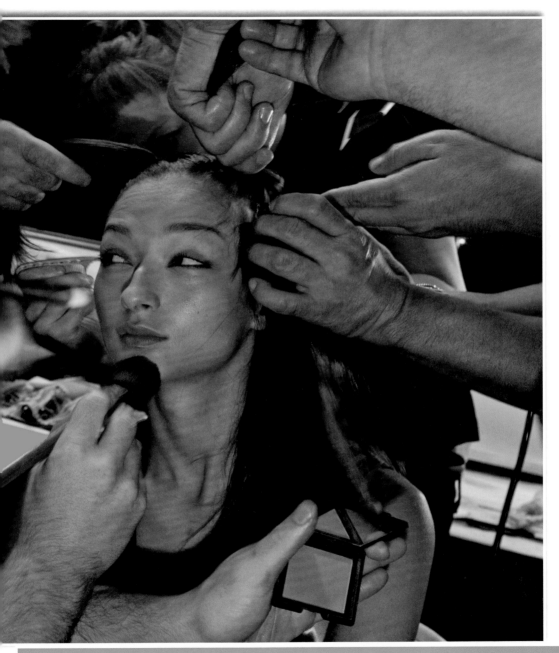

Makeup artists tend to work in the entertainment field. They provide makeup and styling for on-camera or on-stage professionals, such as models, actors, sports personalities, and news broadcasters.

styling), would also broaden your options.

Makeup sales jobs are available at department stores, beauty stores, or stores that sell one brand of product. At these stores, you may offer makeovers, but your primary job is to sell the products. Another option is to work at a salon that specializes in special events, such as weddings and proms. For these occasions, some women have their makeup done professionally. The salons may also offer makeup lessons to customers. These jobs may or may not require a makeup certificate. They definitely require a talent for making people look their best.

Some women are now opting for permanent makeup. Permanent makeup application includes lips, lip liner, eyeliner, mascara, and beauty marks. There are also treatments called micropigmentation that cover tattoos, birthmarks, and scars.

Makeup artists usually travel to the set, bringing their own supplies. They use trusted brands of makeup and also have combs and blow-dryers on hand in case hair styling is required.

Semipermanent treatments include eyelash extensions and tinting, and spray tans. These treatments are offered at specialized salons. Permanent makeup artists usually need special training and certification.

Many makeup artists focus on workers who need professional makeup artistry in their day-to-day jobs: models, actors, television news reporters, and live entertainers. You don't have to live in New York or Los Angeles to find these professionals. Your town likely has advertisers, magazines, and live shows that require makeup artists. These jobs are limited, however, and they are in high demand. Makeup artists in New York and L.A. also face stiff competition and must find an agent first to help them find work. That being said, people appreciate talent, professionalism, people skills, and hard work. If you have these four characteristics, you have a chance of breaking into the field.

Starting out in the field, you may be an assistant at a salon, or if your skills are at a high level, a makeup artist. Your busiest times will be weekends, before weddings and other special occasions. The bustle of people preparing for special moments can be exciting but also stressful. Often these groups are on a tight time schedule and may become impatient if things don't go as planned. For these jobs, it's important to have a cool head. Don't add to the stress by arguing with customers or snapping at coworkers. Stay focused on your clients and making them look beautiful (but do stay on schedule, too). During the week, you may have clients come in to try new makeup, but things will be at a more leisurely pace. You may also opt to do makeup artistry for special occasions on your own, meeting clients at their homes. However, it's a good idea to have a second job lined up, as your clients will likely only need help on Fridays or Saturdays.

JOB SEARCH TOOLS:
WRITING A COVER LETTER AND RÉSUMÉ

A cover letter responds to a job posting and accompanies a résumé. The first paragraph states where you saw the job posting and your interest in the job. The second paragraph highlights skills and experience stated on your résumé, and why they make you a good fit for the company. The final paragraph asks for an interview.

A résumé states your skills and experience relevant to a job. Begin with a profile, or summary of who you are professionally, for example, a licensed cosmetologist with a proven track record of quick and quality work and a can-do and upbeat attitude. Next, state your work experience. Finally, state your education. Under each heading, state skills learned and accomplishments made.

Many books offer examples of letters and résumés. As you read through the examples, you will see how to present your experience and skills in an effective way through your own résumé. You can also get help through your school career counselor or at the library. Be sure to have somebody proofread your cover letter and résumé.

At a department store makeup counter, workers each represent one brand of makeup and skin-care products. You'll likely work next to salespeople representing other brands. You may earn commission—or a percentage—of what you sell. Beauty store makeup artists' jobs are similar, but you may represent more than one brand of makeup. In either place, you can work your way up to manager. There are also jobs with big brands. Merchandisers stock makeup at stores. Sales representatives are assigned a territory. They call on salons or stores to fill product orders and introduce new products. Schedules depend on store and salon hours and when the best time is to meet with customers. Often sales representatives for large companies need a college education, but sales experience and a good track record can also lead to a job. It's important to be great with people and to dress the part; many sales jobs require business attire (suits).

If you plan to do makeup artistry for on-camera professionals, you might start as an assistant. In that case, your schedule would depend on the makeup artist's hours. Tasks may include mixing makeup, prepping a client (by removing makeup and cleansing the face), cleaning brushes, tidying the work area, and scheduling appointments. Eventually, you'll try to be a makeup artist on your own. Clients may include models, actors, magazines, or production companies.

Finally, you may decide to build a freelance business directly after school by networking with photographers, event planners, magazine editors, and others who work with on-camera professionals. To show that you're a talented makeup artist, you'll need to build a book, or portfolio. This will include photos of models whose makeup you've done. You may need to do their makeup for free in order to build your book. If you live in New York or Los Angeles, you'll need an agent to represent you. This also requires a book. While you pursue this work, you'll need reliable income from another job.

Laying the Education Groundwork

While still in high school, it's a good idea to research the qualifications or requirements of the job you desire. That way, you can begin working toward your goal. A good place to start is your library or library Web site. There, you'll find links to both local and national job databases. Choose a database and search the job you desire.

Say you search "makeup artist." Several jobs pop up, including a retail sales job at a makeup counter. This job requires a twelfth-grade education. You now know that some makeup jobs will require high school graduation (as opposed to a GED). Experience in makeup is preferred. A makeup artist or aesthetician license would definitely count as experience. But you may also include makeovers you've done on your own.

Other qualifications include excellent customer service, communication, organization, and time management; a professional demeanor; and a positive attitude. How do you show that you have these skills? Well, first make sure that you do! School may seem like the time to slack off in these areas. But if you stay positive, get your work done on time, and practice professional skills such as looking people in the eyes, dressing your best, and being polite but direct, then you will have the skills you need for the job you seek. Later, you can show that you have these skills through recommendations from

High school is a good time to practice professional skills, such as being on time and being an active participant, and to take basic classes, such as art, math, writing, speech, biology, and chemistry.

teachers and bosses and by how you present yourself during the interview.

While still in high school, you can also begin to take classes that will be helpful to you as a hair stylist or makeup artist. These include:

- **Communication.** Look at any job listing, and you'll see that good communication is a must. Take as many writing and speech classes as you can.
- **Math.** Whether you own your own business or are working for someone else, under-standing your income, taxes, tip percentages, and benefits are a must, and that takes basic accounting knowledge.
- **Business.** If your high school has business classes, this will give you great insight into own-ing a business or being a great employee.

- **Chemistry and biology.** Basic chemistry is helpful in understanding hair treatments and color, and makeup. Biology is helpful in understanding hair and skin.
- **Art.** Makeup and hair styling require an understanding of shape, color, and design. Take as many art classes as you can, and the more hands-on, the better.

For some jobs, a makeup artist needs to have completed a makeup artistry program and may need a license. An aesthetician license is required for jobs in skin care. A hairstylist needs a cosmetology license, which requires completion of cosmetology school. You have several options for school. Your school district may offer vocational programs in cosmetology. These programs are tuition-free and get you on the job after high school. However, not all districts offer programs

When choosing a cosmetology program, you have several options, including a trade school, community college, or vocational program through your school district. Research to find the one that's right for you.

in your area of interest. The second option is a trade school. These schools specialize in hair and beauty. They are sometimes sponsored by salons or beauty product companies. Finally, community colleges often offer courses in hair and makeup.

You may be able to find a trade school or community college with help from a career or guidance counselor. You can also ask friends and acquaintances for recommendations or search the Web. To compare programs, consider tuition, scholarships and financial aid, hours required, public transportation available to the school, and job placement rates. Also learn what job placement services are available. Finally, visit the school to see if it's a good fit for you.

To enroll in a vocational program through your high school, talk to your school counselor. If you've chosen a trade school or community college program, go to the school Web site and follow instructions. The school will likely require an application and your high school transcript or GED score. Be sure to ask how to apply for financial aid if it is available. You can call the school to ensure that it received all the necessary application materials from you.

School Days

Congratulations! You've started school, a big step toward your goals. A lot of people don't realize that their career begins in school. That's because school is a great place to form professional habits and contacts. With that in mind, be friendly and professional to all teachers and classmates.

Dress well. This is especially important in the hair and makeup field. You'll be helping people look their best, so you

JOB SEARCH TOOLS: WRITING AN APPROACH LETTER

An approach letter introduces you to an employer. It is not in response to a job posting, but rather expresses your interest in the company or person. In the first paragraph, state how you heard about the person or company. This may be through a friend or mentor, or through your own research. The second paragraph should state your training, experience, and goal in your field (to become a makeup artist in a special event salon, for instance.) The third paragraph will ask for a meeting to learn more about the company or field. Alternately, you may inquire whether the company is currently accepting résumés.

should look your best, too. You don't need expensive clothes. You just need a style that makes you feel great and look professional. A creative flair is fine in this field, as long as it's not too over the top. However, an inexpensive way to look professional is to wear all black. This attire is common among beauty professionals. It never goes out of style and is flattering to everyone. Plus, it's simple enough that no one will notice if you wear the same few pieces every day.

Show an interest in your studies. Be on time to class and ready to learn. Respond to your teacher's questions and ask questions of your own. Talk to your teacher after class. Show that you plan to do what it takes to succeed in this field. Go the extra mile to keep your work area clean and serve customers in the student salon. Volunteer for jobs within the program, such as organizing a free makeover night.

Collaborate and socialize with classmates. Help them when they are busy or having trouble understanding something. Join study groups and eat lunch with your classmates. Of course, you'll want to avoid drama with other students. When two people feud publicly, nobody remembers who was right or wrong; they only remember that they fought. It's best to either stand your ground calmly or simply walk away. Also, some people seem drawn to drama. Either avoid these people or be careful not to get wrapped up in it. Finally, don't talk badly about people behind their backs. It could get back to them, and even if it doesn't, it paints you in a negative light.

It's also important to stay on top of your studies. Set aside an hour or two to study every day. You can do your homework and review your notes during this time. When you are finished, do

While cosmetology school requires reading, writing, and note taking, much of the work is hands-on. You'll practice hair styling and makeup artistry on mannequins and, later, customers.

independent study—by browsing magazines for style trends or searching job openings, for instance. Before a quiz or test, study what you think will be covered for about an hour. A good way to do this is to take turns quizzing with a friend.

Much of your schoolwork, however, will be hands-on. You'll practice styling mannequins and, later in the program, customers of the school salon. Outside of school, there may be optional practice hours. It's a good idea to attend these, as it shows commitment to the field. And of course, you can never practice too much.

To become certified in your state, you'll need to pass a board exam that includes written and hands-on tests. This may seem daunting now, but your teachers will prepare you for this test. Before the exam, continue with your regular study program, perhaps adding an hour each day. You can find a book with sample tests in your school or local library. The week before, don't stay up late cramming. You need a fresh mind for the test. On the day of the test, take a deep breath. Remember that you are well prepared, and know that people typically score well on tests when they are interested in the subject matter. If you experience test anxiety, talk to a school counselor before the test.

After passing your boards, the next step is to achieve certification through your state board. This will require some paperwork. If you have a question about what is required, check the Web site, talk to a teacher or fellow student, or call the board and ask. Note that you'll need to be licensed in the state in which you work. If you plan to move out of state after school, check that state cosmetology board's Web site to learn the requirements.

Now it's time to bridge the gap between school and career. You may find a mentor in your field, somebody who offers advice on navigating your career. This could be a teacher, boss, coworker, family member, or friend in the field. By demonstrating hard work, willingness to learn, and good communication, you show that his or her time will be well spent on you. Another good bridge to employment is an internship in your field. Finally, you can learn on the job, an option that offers the obvious benefit of getting paid. For any of these options, you'll need a solid résumé and cover letter.

Researching Job Openings

Now it's time to find your first job in your field. Before applying for jobs, have a cover letter, a résumé, a list of at least three references, three letters of recommendation, proof of board certification, and school transcripts ready. Ask teachers, former bosses, mentors, or people for whom you have volunteered if they would write letters of recommendation. Ask if they would also be willing to be listed as references (in which case a person from the salon may call them). If they agree, be sure to write down their contact information. Some applications ask for references and others ask for letters of recommendation, so it's important to have both. Have these materials saved on a flash drive so that you can work on computers at the library or at school.

Also, you need to decide what is essential to you in a job. That may include location, in which case you'll search jobs only in your city. You may also only be interested in full-time jobs. Now you can begin your search online through a job database. Have a goal in mind, for instance, to apply for three jobs per day. Focus on jobs for which you are qualified. The list of qualifications is

Networking is an important part of finding a job. You can network at job fairs, among friends and family, and with fellow graduates of your cosmetology program.

the bare minimum you need to be considered for the job. Many jobs will allow you to apply online. Fill out applications completely and neatly, using proper spelling and grammar. Be sure to include any requested transcripts or certifications. Also, be sure to attach your cover letter and résumé, if possible. Tailor the cover letter to each salon by addressing the salon by name. Call the salon to find out to whom the letter should be addressed. If an application needs to be filled out by hand, use your best handwriting. When you deliver the application, be sure to dress and act professionally. Employers often ask receptionists their impression of the person who filled out the application.

Know that not all available jobs are listed. If there is a salon where you'd like to work, find the company online, call to ask who does the hiring, and send a cover letter and résumé. You can also research new salons in the area by reading local business news online. New salons often need new stylists. If you apply, you can mention in your cover letter seeing the article.

This may sound a bit daunting. Job help centers at your school or the public library can help you write a résumé and cover letter, search for jobs, and fill out an application. Find out if there is a class available or if you need to set an appointment. Decide what you would like to learn from your appointment, and schedule a follow-up if needed.

When searching for a job, be careful not to go through the motions. Online research is just one avenue. Personal connections can be more important. A way to meet many employers at once is by attending career fairs. Some career fairs focus on beauty jobs. Others are more general. If you attend a career fair, have a game plan. List your favorite

USING SOCIAL MEDIA FOR NETWORKING: DO'S AND DON'TS

Do: Share milestones. People root for those who pursue their goals through hard work. They will be excited for you on your first day of school, first day on the job, etc. And if they hear of an opening in your field, they'll think of you.

Don't: Complain about school or work. Everybody has to wake up in the morning, handle boring situations and difficult people, and sometimes work into the night. Nobody likes to hear others complain about it.

Do: Show your expertise, such as photos of work you've done or links to products and styles you like. People like hearing expert advice, and when they need a stylist, they'll think of you.

Don't: Forget to ask permission before posting pictures of customers. (You'll find that many people will be happy to be photographed after a day at the salon.) Also, ask your employer about any social media guidelines.

Do: Connect with classmates and teachers via social media. If you think it's appropriate, you can also connect with customers.

Don't: Complain about customers or colleagues online, even if you don't name them. When people read these thoughts, they think, "Well, if I go to her as a hairstylist, I'll be complained about."

companies, what job you would like, and why you are qualified. When you talk to representatives, listen to what their companies need. Then state in a couple of sentences why you would be a good fit. Take a card. Follow up with an e-mail and attached résumé.

Job Opportunities Are Everywhere: Even at the Family Picnic

It's also important to make career connections in less obvious places. About half of all open jobs are not advertised. Instead they are filled through word of mouth. Think about it: if you were seeking a hairstylist for yourself, wouldn't you choose somebody you knew or who a friend recommended? That's how employers think, too.

You've already done some networking while in school. Stay in touch with your teachers and classmates. Let teachers know of your goals and progress in your job search. Knowing the direction of your search, they may think of other places to try. Classmates can share information about job openings and offer moral support as you seek jobs together. Outside of school, friends and family can help you to meet people in your career. That means you should put your best foot forward at family reunions, church gatherings, and everywhere you go. Just as you were in school, be friendly and positive about yourself,

Stay in touch with classmates after school. You can offer moral support to each other as you search for jobs. You can also share information about job openings.

others, and your field. When people ask how school or the job search is going, always answer in a positive light.

You may think this sounds fake or phony. You may ask, "Why can't I just be myself?" Of course, you can be yourself. And you should be. Be you at your most confident and open to opportunities. For instance, if you're not outgoing, you don't need to "work the room," shaking hands with everybody. Eye contact and a smile show that you're open to conversation. On the other hand, if you have a fun personality, you don't have to become Miss Buttoned-Up Professional. You can continue to be fun, but also express your career goals and what you're doing to achieve them.

If it comes up in the conversation, express your specific goals. If you say that you want to do makeup, the person will just nod and say that's nice. But if you state that you'd like to do makeup for print media, he or she may say, "Oh, I know a magazine editor you should talk to." Finally, be the expert in hair and makeup for those you know. This means sharing information. For instance, on social media, you can share products and styles you like. First

You can also network through trade organizations, at trade shows, and by taking cosmetology classes outside of school. Do a search on the Internet to find out more about classes near you.

people may only ask you for personal advice ("What color lipstick should I be wearing?"). But soon, you'll find that they're connecting you to people they know or coming to you as their beauty professional.

It's important not to be pushy, always asking people to connect you or make a phone call. Instead, have a normal, back-and-forth conversation. People like to help. If they sense your enthusiasm and commitment, they'll likely help however they can.

Many friends and family members will know at least one person in the beauty field: their own hairstylists. However, you may need to expand the pool of people you know in order to meet somebody who is hiring. You can do this by joining trade associations and attending beauty classes and conferences. If you know whom you would like to work for, go the extra mile to see if anyone you know or any alumni from your program work there. Talk to them to learn more about the company. Later, if a position opens, you will have a contact at the salon. But don't set your heart on just one company. Find five others similar to that salon, and also pursue jobs there. Finally, you can seek internships at companies, which will help you to gain experience and meet people in the field and may lead to a job at the company.

CHAPTER FOUR

Preparing for the Interview

Through your networking and research, you'll find individuals to contact. If they are hiring, you can ask to interview for the job. If they aren't hiring, you can ask for an informational meeting. You can ask how they got their foot in the door or what experience is needed to work there. You may also get interviews through your applications. Because employers often call to set up interviews, be sure to answer your cell phone professionally and to have a good outgoing message. Also have a professional sounding e-mail address.

Getting an interview is a big step, and you should be proud of yourself. You also have a lot of preparation to do. First, think about why you want this job. Beyond the obvious—that you enjoy doing hair or makeup—you may also like talking to people and seeing their confidence improve when they look their best. Also think about why you'd like to work for this employer. Do they specialize in weddings, and you'd like to help people on this special day? Do they have a great training program? Do their stylists have a reputation for being on the cutting edge?

Next, think about what would make you an asset to this employer. For instance, you may have been the student other students turned to for advice on color. You may have specialized in updos at the student salon. Or perhaps you have

Enthusiasm for the job shows in an interview. Why would you like to work at that particular salon? Perhaps the salon specializes in special events, like weddings or other formal affairs.

experience styling curly hair because everybody in your family has curly hair. Also think about your personality: Are you personable? Do you exude a sense of calm that customers appreciate? Are you a go-getter who was always planning events while in school? Try to think of times when these characteristics were helpful to those around you.

Learn about your potential employer by visiting the company Web site, reading articles, or talking to others. Know their specialty services and top products. If possible, learn what customers say about them. Think about a few questions you could ask—things you're genuinely interested in knowing. For instance: "About how many wedding parties do you handle per weekend?"

Finally, prepare to answer the interview questions. Ask a friend from your cosmetology program to practice interviewing with you. The interview may include:

• Questions about you, such as "Tell me about yourself." Be prepared to say a few sentences about your personal, educational, and work background. This is your opportunity to show your positive personality and commitment to the beauty field. You might say, "I grew up here in Omaha, the youngest of four children. I was always doing their hair. When I began cosmetology school, I

You can practice interviewing with a friend. Learn common questions and have answers prepared. But also be ready to answer unexpected questions. Just be your most positive self.

could tell it was a perfect fit." You may be asked what your classmates would say about you. This is your chance to state the talents and personality you bring to a work environment. It's also common to be asked about strengths and weaknesses. The weakness question is tricky. It's important to share a genuine weakness, not something like "I work too hard; I care too much," which sounds cheesy. At the same time, you never want to share a weakness that will affect your chance at getting the job, such as, "I'm always running late." It's a good idea to share a weakness based on your experience level and to state what you're doing about it. Other questions may concern career goals. Share your goals for right now and your goals for five years from now.

• Experience questions: These questions focus on the skills you have learned and proven through experience. The interviewer may say, "Tell me about your experience with makeup artistry for events," or "Tell me about a time you were a leader." The questions may focus on how you handled problems: "Tell me about a time you dealt with a difficult customer." If you have never faced that problem, it's OK to say that and to answer what you would do if that problem arose.

• Scenario questions: These are similar to experience questions, but they ask about problems that may arise on the job. The interviewer may ask, "What would you do if it was a busy day at the salon and all the hairstylists needed your help?" It's OK to take a minute to think about your answers. Then you can state the steps you would take to solve the problem.

STYLIST TO THE STARS

Have you ever wondered who styles hair or does makeup for magazines, TV, and movies? These professionals usually start as assistants while also working at a salon. They choose either print (magazines) or TV and movies. They may also specialize in live shows. As assistants, they build their portfolios. That is, they put together a book of photos that show their work. They may include pages from magazines—photos of models who they helped style. These are called tear sheets. Based on these photos, they are hired to do their own work. Then they find an agent who helps them find more work. This is a competitive field that requires a lot of hustle. But with the right attitude and talent, it's possible to break in.

Further Preparations

It's time to get ready for the interview. Choose an outfit that you would wear on a dressy day at work. For a hairstyling or makeup artist job, you might wear a fashionable black dress, with your hair and makeup done well, but simply. While this is a creative field, it's best not to have your hair or makeup too creative, or the employer might think that's the only style you can do. You want the employer to know that you can do a wide variety of styles. (You can also talk to other students and teachers about what to wear.)

Now it's time to gather what you'll need. This includes your résumé, references, certification, transcript, and a

Being on time to an interview is essential. Set an alarm and also have a friend call you to make sure you are awake. Allow extra time in case something goes wrong.

portfolio of your work, which you will have built during school. Being on time is essential. The day before the interview, make a test run so that you know the best route and how long it takes. Get lots of sleep the night before. If the interview is earlier than you usually wake up, be sure to set your alarm. You may even want to schedule a backup call from a friend. You'll want to be twenty minutes early to the interview. Because traffic can be slow and buses can run late, you should shoot for being thirty minutes early. If you are too early, find a spot a little off-site and read or prepare for your interview until you're only twenty minutes early.

Your first interview may be over the phone. In that case, practice over the phone with a friend. Ask her how you sounded. Phone interviews can be challenging because the interviewer can't see that you're dressed professionally, sitting up straight, and looking her in the eye. You have to demonstrate your confidence and friendliness by your voice alone. One way to do this is by smiling because a smile can be "heard" over the phone. Also, practice speaking directly and loudly enough with your friend. It's still OK to pause to think about your answers, but say, "Let me think about that for a minute" so that the interviewer doesn't think the call has been dropped. When the time comes, ensure a quiet place to answer the phone. Smile and do your best.

CHAPTER FIVE

The Interview

Think of an interview as meeting someone new. Not everybody is going to become your best friend. But it can still be fun and worthwhile to meet new people. Likewise, not every interview is going to result in a job. But talking to the interviewer can be fun and worthwhile anyway. Hopefully, this attitude will take the pressure off you and allow you to enjoy the process. It's an exciting time: the start of your career.

The interview actually starts on your commute. Be courteous. People headed to the same place often see each other on the road. You don't want to cut off your interviewer in traffic or ace the interviewer out of a seat on the subway. When you arrive, be courteous in the parking lot, entrance, and elevator. Smile and hold doors for others. Be friendly to the receptionist, but avoid the temptation to overshare because of nervousness. You want to make a more professional impression than that. Let the receptionist know that you are early and can wait.

When your interviewer greets you, offer a firm handshake and make eye contact. Good posture and a smile will make you appear relaxed and confident, even if you are nervous. Listen politely and speak directly. Be yourself. If your purse falls or you stumble over a sentence, it's OK to smile and take a deep breath. You're only human.

The interview usually begins with small talk. This is an important part of the interview. Offer more than yes or no answers. For example, if the interviewer asks, "Did you have a

A job interview begins on your commute and carries into the parking lot, waiting area, and elevator. You never know where you will first see your potential employer, and a good first impression is important.

nice weekend?" answering, "Yes," is a dead end. Try something like: "Yes, I babysat for my sister's children and took them to the zoo. We saw the new polar bear." Now the interviewer can talk about babysitting, the zoo, or the polar bear. This keeps the conversation going. Even if you did nothing exciting, you can mention that you had a quiet weekend and got things organized around the house. This is also the time to relax and get into listening mode. Listen to the questions first. Then, think about what you want to say. If you think about it while she is talking, you may miss part of the question.

Now the planned interview begins. The interviewer is trying to determine whether you would be a good fit for the company. She already thinks this is possible, which is why she scheduled the interview. So in a sense, she is on your side. However, employees that are difficult to work with or who don't have the necessary experience can be a liability. The interviewer is screening you to make sure you don't fall into either category. At the same time, there are other candidates for the job. Among the good candidates, the interviewer is trying to determine the best person for the job.

Answer the interview questions by identifying what the employer needs and how you can meet that need. For instance, if asked how you would handle the fast pace of a salon that specializes in weddings, you could say, "I know that you have a busy bridal business on the weekends. In our practice studio, I was one of the fastest workers, and my customers were very happy with the results. I also worked as a waitress in a busy restaurant, and I didn't get rattled. I like fast-paced work environments."

You can also tell a short story to illustrate a point. For instance, if asked how you dealt with a difficult customer, you could say, "I dealt with an unhappy customer at the restaurant

You may be asked in an interview how you handled difficult situations at an old job. Describe only situations in which you brought about a positive outcome.

where I worked. The lunch wait was two hours, and she was upset. I said that I could put her name at the top of the list for dinner. She decided to come back then." Only tell stories in which things ended well. Save horror stories for your close friends!

Ask questions whenever it comes naturally. During small talk, you may ask how many people the interviewer has spoken with today. You might ask a question related to the company, such as how long they've been in their present location. You may also try to clarify a question that is asked of you. Avoid sensitive or nosy questions, and don't discuss salary unless the interviewer brings it up. If she asks what you would like to make, be prepared to say a typical starting salary in your field.

At the end of interview, let the interviewer know that you are still interested in the position. You could say, "I'm very interested in this position, and I appreciate you interviewing me." When you get home, write a thank-you note and mail it right away. Then, call to

THROUGH THE INTERVIEWER'S EYES

While the interviewer asks you questions, she is trying to answer the following questions for herself:

- Would this person make a good impression on customers? This is determined by your professional dress and style and how you carry yourself.

- Would he or she be enjoyable to work with? This is determined by the small talk at the beginning and end of the interview and your overall demeanor.

- Would he or she be able to do the job? This is determined through questions about your experience.

- Will he or she enjoy this job? Employers ask questions about why you entered the field and why you want to work for this employer.

- Will he or she take the initiative to help customers, coworkers, and the business? Employers will ask for examples of how you showed leadership, initiative, or cooperation while still in school.

- Is he or she a good communicator? Employers can tell this by how you handle the interview.

- Can he or she handle a difficult situation? Employers ask how you have handled problems in the past.

- Does he or she have outside interests? This shows general enthusiasm and is usually determined through small talk or questions like, "What do you enjoy doing outside of work?"

follow up in a week or two. If you learn that you didn't get the job, respond politely. You may ask what you could improve in terms of your interview skills. You can also ask her to consider you if another position opens. Remember, it takes only one yes to get a job, and the number of nos do not matter in the end.

Do's and Don'ts

During the interview, you may be nervous. Many people have the tendency to overshare in these circumstances. Promise yourself in advance not to say the following ten things during an interview, no matter what:

1. Anything bad or confessional about yourself.
2. Anything negative about another person. While answering a question about dealing with a difficult person, you may have to slightly bend this rule. However, be as understanding of the person as possible in your response. Also, only describe instances when you handled a difficult person well. Everybody has lost their patience, but now is not the time to share that.
3. Any personal challenge that ended poorly. Everybody also has a story in which he or she did not rise to the occasion, but now is not the time to share that, either.
4. Anything negative about the company. Never imply that you are needed to fix a problem. Example: "I think your hairstylists are behind the times. I can bring the latest styles to your customers." That's just impolite.

5. Anything negative about another salon. It's a small world, and the interviewer could be friends with people at that salon. And if not, he or she may wonder if you'll speak badly of this salon, too.

6. Anything that suggests you will want special privileges. Don't ask about holidays or days off during the interview. That can be addressed at the time of hiring.

7. Anything that suggests you'll focus on what the job will offer you instead of what you can offer this job.

8. That you won't be on time or able to show up reliably.

9. That you would be dramatic or difficult to get along with.

10. Bad language, excessive slang, or improper grammar.

On the other hand, you *should* try to share these ten things:

1. Your enthusiasm about the job.

2. Your confidence that you can do the job.

3. Examples of when you were a leader.

4. Examples of when you solved a problem or overcame a challenge.

5. What you will bring to the table.

6. Specific tools and training you have.

Being offered an interview shows that the employer is interested in hiring you. Stay positive, and be your best self. If you don't get the job, the interview was still good practice.

7. Specific experience you have.

8. Something that made you stand out in school.

9. Transferable skills from other jobs. (This may be your first job in your field, but other jobs were good experience. Were you a hostess at a restaurant? Then you have experience working with the public and with staff. Did you work in a daycare? Then you have experience with children and with being patient.)

10. Thank the interviewer for her time.

During your interviews, be genuine, but present the very best version of yourself. It's not being dishonest; it's being professional. Think of it this way: when at work, you'll need to be your most polished self, so present yourself that way in the interview. If one interview goes poorly, chalk it up to experience. You can learn from the interview and do better on the next one.

CHAPTER SIX

Getting Hired and Beyond

Congratulations! You've been offered your first job. Quick, quick say yes! Actually, don't. You need to gather more information. First, are there interviewers who haven't contacted you yet? Now is the time to follow up. Let them know you have an offer and ask if they've made a hiring decision. You need to know your options before making a decision.

Interested employers will offer you a specific salary and benefits. You can negotiate these, by say, asking for $2,000 more per year. That adds up over the years. As for benefits, you can sometimes negotiate for an extra week of paid time off. This is a good idea if you have family obligations that require occasional time off. Keep in mind that your pay arrangement may be based on commission. Find out what the base pay is. (Employers are required to pay at least minimum wage, even if you work on commission.)

Also, ask yourself if you really want this job. While at the interview, you may have noticed unhappy employees, slow business, or some indication of company turmoil. In that case, consider your options. If this is your only offer, decide whether you can afford to continue your job search. If you already have a job outside your field, you might keep that job and continue to look. However, if you are unemployed, you might

Most coworkers will be fun and helpful, and getting to know them will be one of the best aspects of the job. But expect a few difficult coworkers and plan to handle them in a positive manner.

decide to take this job while giving yourself a year to find a new job. It will provide you with experience and income.

Let's say, however, that you're truly excited about this job. What can you expect on your first day? Ask your interviewer where to go when you arrive. Get there early and be ready to meet lots of new people. Know who your supervisors are and learn as many of your coworkers' names as possible. Show that you plan to be a capable, considerate, and helpful member of the team. You may spend your first day going through orientation and filling out paperwork. At orientation, you will learn more about your benefits and pay. You may choose your health insurance plan. Be sure to read the options carefully to determine what plan works best for you now. Also ask when you are able to change plans, as your situation may change. You can choose the amount of taxes you would like withheld from each paycheck. Financially, it is better to have fewer taxes withheld. That way, you can earn interest by keeping your own money in a savings or checking account. However, if receiving a lump sum in April helps you to plan for large expenses, you might choose to have more taxes withheld.

You may also be able to contribute to your 401k. This is your retirement fund. Retirement might seem far off, but the earlier you contribute, the more you'll have when you can no longer work. The 401k money is also available in case of emergency (though financial experts would advise against tapping into it). Many companies match the amount you give. This is free money, so try to contribute the maximum amount matched.

After orientation, you may receive training. You'll likely shadow another stylist while he or she offers information

You'll likely announce your new job on social media. Be sure to maintain a positive and professional persona, especially in regards to what you share about work.

and advice. The owner or manager may also give you a tour of the salon. If no training is offered, ask your supervisor for a tour of the workplace and schedule a meeting at the end of your first day so that you can ask questions.

With training complete, work begins. Now, you'll get to know coworkers and customers. You'll become familiar with the workspace and routines. You'll also learn how lunch and other breaks work. Be sure to take a lunch or dinner break. It may seem like a time saver to skip it, but in the long run you'll be more energized and efficient.

Once you settle in, you'll want to announce your job to your family and friends. You may also share your good news on Facebook or through a group e-mail. Be sure to let people know how to schedule appointments if you are taking new clients. You'll also want to let your school, teachers, and classmates know of your job. It's important to stay in touch with these contacts, even once you have a job.

Beyond the First Day

Succeeding in your new workplace will be similar to succeeding in school. You'll want to be friendly with your coworkers and supervisors while avoiding drama. However, instead of having a teacher, you now have a boss. Your teacher's primary job was to help students succeed. But your boss has other responsibilities. Some bosses are hands-on managers and mentors to their workers. Others work behind the scenes. In that case, you may seek help or advice from a more experienced hair stylist. Over time, that person may become your mentor. Your salon may also have a mentorship program as part of your training. Even if your boss works behind the scenes, try to forge a working relationship. When your boss asks, "How are things going?" Rather than saying, "Great," add a specific example of why things are going great. That way, he or she will know that you're making a positive impact on the company.

Not every day will go smoothly, and problems may arise with coworkers. Handle these problems by stating your point of view tactfully. Many of your coworkers will become friends. However, you may have a coworker who is consistently rude. Don't stoop to that level or assume that he or she speaks for everyone. If you observe closely, you might find that this person is simply difficult. If the problem is truly affecting your work, or the salon's business, discuss your specific concerns with the person. If he or she doesn't listen, you may need to talk to your boss. But it may be best to ignore this person instead.

You will likely enjoy most of your customers. People tend to be relaxed and happy on beauty days. It's also an opportunity for them to share what's going on in their lives. Be sure to keep what they tell you in confidence. You may also have some difficult customers. If you treat them kindly, and meet their reasonable demands (even if these go beyond the call of duty), you may find that that they aren't so bad after all. More commonly, you'll have tricky situations with typically easygoing customers. Somebody might get impatient and want her hair done in a hurry or dislike her hairstyle. Most hairstylists will redo a hairstyle that a customer dislikes. But it's important to be firm in other areas, such as scheduling, so that your business runs smoothly.

Life is all about managing expectations. If you accept that on some days you will be mistreated, ignored, or inconvenienced by a coworker or customer, you'll be able to handle it calmly and hold your head high at the end of the day. Be

COMMISSION VS. BOOTH RENTAL

Commission employees earn a percentage of what they bring in through their appointments. You typically earn 30-45 percent of the appointment cost, and keep the entire tip. So if a $100 hair appointment took two hours, you would earn approximately $40, or $20 per hour. If in the next hour, you had no appointment, that average would go down. For each paycheck, the employer is required to pay you at least minimum wage, even if you did not earn that through commissions. This provides a safety net for you as you build your clientele. Under a commission arrangement, you typically receive benefits, paid time off, and training. You must follow salon rules, which may include a set shift and dress code.

Booth rental is equivalent to owning your own business. You keep your earnings and pay rent to the salon. You are responsible for buying your own supplies and paying your own taxes. The salon owner is not required to compensate you if you do not earn minimum wage. On the other hand, you set your own schedule and wear what you like. Because of the financial risk involved, most cosmetologists do not begin their careers renting booths.

sure to have a network of friends and family outside of work to help you put such days in perspective.

No matter how much you love your job, at the end of two weeks, your paycheck is important. With your career on track, you're probably thinking about your budget. Experts say to save 10 percent of every paycheck. This money is set aside for emergencies. With the rest of your paycheck, you can pay for necessary expenses and fun stuff. To know how much you can spend on each, make a list of all of your expenses

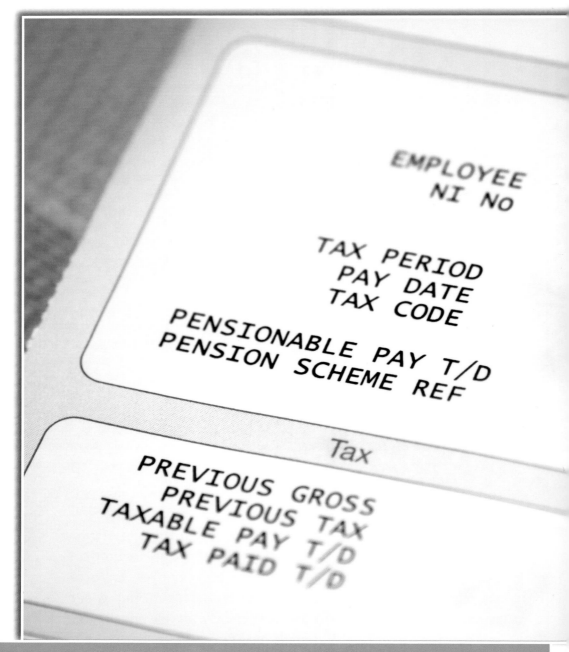

EMPLOYEE
NI NO

TAX PERIOD
PAY DATE
TAX CODE

PENSIONABLE PAY T/D
PENSION SCHEME REF

Tax

PREVIOUS GROSS
PREVIOUS TAX
TAXABLE PAY T/D
TAX PAID T/D

With your career on track, it's time to budget. It's important to save a little of each paycheck so that you can handle emergencies and work toward long-range goals, such as owning a car.

for one month. Divide them into two categories: wants and needs. In the needs category, list rent, utilities, food, and transportation. If you have family obligations, you'll list those expenses, too. In the wants category, list things like movies, going out with friends, and clothes. Now add up your occasional expenses for the year. These may include yearly dues for professional organizations, birthday and holiday presents, and your own beauty appointments. Divide this list by twelve. That amount should be added to your monthly expenses. Do the three lists combined equal what's left of your paycheck after savings? If not, you need to reduce one or all of the lists, work overtime, or get a second job.

After a year of work, you may ask for an annual review. In this meeting, your boss will offer positive comments and constructive criticism. You can also present accomplishments you've made in your first year and what your goals are for next year. If things have gone well, you may ask for a raise. Be sure to support your specific request with evidence of how you have helped the company.

After your first year of work, future goals will become clear. Consider your options and think about the steps you can take to achieve them.

Never ask for a raise because you personally need one.

By now, you probably have a clear picture of your workplace. If you enjoy working there, start thinking of ways to move up. If you are an assistant, think about how to become a stylist. This is something you can ask your boss during your review. On the other hand, you might decide that this isn't where you want to spend your career. Decide what else you want to accomplish at this job. At the same time, begin looking for other opportunities. When you start applying for new jobs, be discreet. You usually don't let your current boss know of your desire to leave until you are offered another job. When you do leave, give your boss time to fill your position, and offer to train the new employee. Try to maintain a positive relationship with your current boss and coworkers, as you'll likely encounter them again in the world of beauty.

GLOSSARY

aesthetician A cosmetologist that focuses on skin-care services, such as facials.

assistant A worker who helps a more experienced worker. In positions where learning is emphasized, the term "apprentice" is sometimes used.

barber A worker trained in haircutting, hair styling, and shaving.

beautician A worker trained in the cosmetology arts; usually called a cosmetologist today.

board certification An official document stating that a person completed the necessary education and tests required to do a particular job.

booth rental Paying a salon for the use of a booth. In this case, the cosmetologist is paid directly by clients.

commission An agreed upon percentage of total sales that is paid to a worker.

community college A school that offers certificate programs, such as cosmetology, and class credits that can be transferred to a four-year college.

cosmetologist A worker trained in hairstyling, manicures, pedicures, waxing, facials, and makeup art.

freelance Describes services sold to buyers on a job-by-job basis.

hairstylist A cosmetologist specializing in hair care.

job database An online collection of job openings.

makeup artist A specialist in applying makeup.

mentor An experienced worker who helps a less experienced worker navigate his or her career.

nail technology An area of cosmetology focusing on manicures and pedicures.

networking The act of forming professional relationships and sharing career information with those you meet.

permanent makeup Lasting pigmentation applied to the face for cosmetic effect.

portfolio A collection of samples of a person's work, such as photographs of hairstyles a hairstylist has done.

qualifications The necessary experience and skills required for a particular job.

résumé A document stating educational, career, and volunteer experience, prepared by a job seeker to share with employers.

salon A business that offers beauty services, such as hairstyling.

shampooer A salon assistant that prepares a client for hairstyling.

vocational program A course of study that prepares students to start their careers after high school.

Aesthetics International Association
310 E. Interstate 30, Suite B107
Garland, TX 75043
(877) 968-7539
Web site: http://www.aestheticsassociation.com
The Aesthetics International Association promotes education, standardized licensing, and networking and learning opportunities for aestheticians.

Allied Beauty Association
145 Traders Boulevard East, Units 26 and 27
Mississauga, ON L4Z3L3
Canada
(905) 568-0158
Web site: http://www.abacanada.com
The Allied Beauty Association, formed in 1934, represents Canadian professionals in the beauty supply industry. It also hosts trade shows and competitions for hairstylists throughout Canada.

American Board of Certified Haircolorists
P.O. Box 9090
San Pedro, CA 90734
(310) 547-0814
E-mail: andre@haircolorist.com
Web site: http://www.haircolorist.com
The American Board of Certified Haircolorists offers certification in hair coloring to stylists.

Associated Skin Care Professionals
25188 Genesee Trail Road, Suite 200

Golden, CO 80401
(800) 789-0411
Web site: http://ascpskincare.com
Associated Skin Care Professionals is the largest professional membership organization for skin care
professionals.

Cosmetology Industry Association of British Columbia
899 West 8th Avenue
Vancouver, BC V5Z 1E3
Canada
(604) 871-0222
Web site: http://www.ciabc.net
The Cosmetology Industry Association of British Columbia
is an organization for beauty professionals.

Nails, Skin & Hair of America
P.O. Box 679
Aiken, SC 29802
Phone: 803.226.0357
Fax: 803.642.0325
E-mail: nailsskinhair@gmail.com
Web site: http://www.nailsskinhair.org
Nails, Skin & Hair of America provides networking and
education opportunities, including online courses.

National Cosmetology Association
401 N. Michigan Avenue
Chicago, IL 60611
(866) 871-0656
Web site: http://www.probeauty.org

The National Cosmetology Association represents the interests of salon owners, hairstylists, nail technicians, aestheticians, and others in the beauty industry.

National Latino Cosmetology Association
7925 W Russell Rd # 401285
Las Vegas, NV   89140
Telephone: 877.658.3801
E-mail: info@nlcamerican.org
Web site: http://www.nlcamerican.org
The National Latino Cosmetology Association provides networking and educational opportunities to Latino beauty and spa professionals.

United Food and Commercial Workers International Union (UFCW)
1775 K Street NW
Washington, DC 20006
(202) 223-3111
Web site: http://www.ufcw.org
The UFCW is the union that represents barbers and beauticians.

Web Sites

Due to the changing nature of Internet links, Rosen Publishing has developed an online list of Web sites related to the subject of this book. This site is updated regularly. Please use this link to access the list:

http://www.rosenlinks.com/JOBS/Hair

Brown, Bobbi. *Bobbi Brown Makeup Manual: For Everyone from Beginner to Pro.* New York, NY: Hachette, 2011.

Christen, Carol, and Richard Bolles. *What Color Is Your Parachute? For Teens.* Berkeley, CA: Ten Speed Press, 2010.

Davis, Gretchen. *The Makeup Artist Handbook, Second Edition: Techniques for Film, Television, Photography, and Theatre.* New York, NY: Focal Press, 2012.

Dennis, Mary. *Careers in Cosmetology* (Success Without College). Hauppauge, NY: Barron's, 2000.

Farr, Michael, and Laurence Shatkin. *300 Best Jobs Without a Four-Year Degree.* St. Paul, MN: JIST, 2009.

Ferguson Publishing. *Careers in Focus: Cosmetology.* 4th ed. New York, NY: Ferguson Publishing, 2008.

Gearhart, Susan. *Opportunities in Beauty and Modeling Careers.* Columbus, OH: McGraw-Hill, 2004.

Heos, Bridget. *A Career as a Hairstylist.* (Essential Careers). New York, NY: Rosen, 2011.

Iman. *The Beauty of Color: The Ultimate Beauty Guide for Skin of Color.* New York, NY: Perigee, 2006.

James, Jennifer. *FabJob Guide to Become a Makeup Artist.* Calgary, Canada: FabJob.com, 2005.

Jones, Robert. *Makeup Makeovers: Weddings: Stunning Looks for the Entire Bridal Party.* Minneapolis, MN: Fair Winds, 2006.

Kidd, Jemma. *Makeup Master Class.* New York, NY: St. Martin's, 2009.

Milady. *Professional Management for Men: Career Management for Barbers.* Albany, NY: Milady, 2006.

Peterson's. *Teen's Guide to College and Career Success: Your High School Roadmap for College & Career Success* (Teen's Guide to College and Career Planning). 10th ed. Albany, NY: Peterson's, 2008.

Shamboosie. *Beautiful Black Hair: Real Solutions to Real Problems—A Step by Step Instructional Guide.* Phoenix, AZ: Amber Communications, 2002.

Troutman, Kathryn Kraemer. *Creating Your High School Résumé: A Step-By-Step Guide to Preparing an Effective Résumé for Jobs, College, and Training Programs.* St. Paul, MN: JIST Publishing, 2003.

Vetica, Robert. *Good to Great Hair.* Beverly, MA: Fair Winds Press, 2009.

Worthington, Charles. *The Complete Book of Hairstyling.* Ontario, Canada: Firefly Books, 2002.

Wright, Crystal. *Crystal Wright's Hair Makeup & Fashion Styling Career Guide.* Avon, MA: Adams Media, 2009.

Yate, Martin. *Knock 'em Dead Résumés.* 8th Ed. Avon, MA: Adams Media, 2008.

Allen, Jeffrey. *Instant Interviews*. Hoboken, NJ: John Wiley & Sons, 2009.

Asher, Donald. *How to Get Any Job*. Berkeley, CA: Ten Speed, 2009

Beshara, Tony. *Acing the Interview*. New York, NY: AMACOM, 2008.

Bureau of Labor Statistics. "Barbers, Hairdressers, and Cosmetologists." Retrieved July 10, 2012 (http://www .bls.gov/ooh/personal-care-and-service/barbers -hairdressers-and-cosmetologists.htm).

Farrel, Maureen. "How to Run a Beauty Salon: Costs." *Forbes*. April 20, 2007. Retrieved August 25, 2012 (http://www .forbes.com/2007/04/20/beauty-salon-aniston-ent-fin -cx_mf_0420fundsalonexpenses.html).

Figler, Howard. *The Complete Job-Search Handbook*. New York, NY: Holt, 1999.

Gentile, India. Author interview. September 14, 2009.

Hawk, Barbara. *What Employers Really Want*. Chicago, IL: VGM, 1998.

IRS. *Cosmetology: Learning the Art of Doing Business. Instructor's Guide*. Washington, DC: IRS, 2004.

Korman, Lorraine, with Felice Pimeau Devine. *Cosmetology Career Starter*. 2nd ed. New York, NY: Learning Express, 2002.

Lamb, Catherine. *Milady's Life Management Skills for Cosmetology, Barber-Styling, and Nail Technology*. Albany, NY: Milady, 1996.

McKinney, Anne. *Real-Résumés for Retailing, Modeling, Fashion & Beauty Jobs*. Fayetteville, NC: Prep Pub, 2012.

Milady. *Milady's Standard Cosmetology*. Albany, NY: Milady, 2008.

Pankalla, Anita. Author interview. July 22, 2009.

Pivot Point. *Salon Fundamentals.* Evanston, IL: Pivot Point, 2000.

Ramirez, Laurie. Author interview. September 5, 2012.

Robertson, Lindsay. Author interview. July 22, 2009.

Wright, Crystal. *The Hair, Makeup & Styling Career Guide.* 2nd ed. Los Angeles, CA: Pace Publishing Group, 1994.

S

salary, negotiating, 57
sales representatives for
    makeup companies, 17–18
shampooer/assistant hair
    stylist, 7–8
skin care/skin-care treatments,
    12, 22
social media, 36, 61
  networking and, 33
specialized salons, 14–16
state boards of barbering and
    cosmetology, 7

T

tear sheets, 44
thank-you notes, 51
tips, 8
trade associations, 38
trade schools, 24

V

vocational programs,
    22, 24

About the Author

Bridget Heos is the author of more than forty young adult and children's nonfiction books. She lives in Kansas City with her husband and their three sons.

Photo Credits